AF269337

What You Weren't Told

A Parent's Guide to Raising Kids Who Love to Read

Michelle Gomes

Red Thread Publishing LLC. 2023

Write to info@redthreadbooks.com if you are interested in publishing with Red Thread Publishing. Learn more about publications or foreign rights acquisitions of our catalog of books: www.redthreadbooks.com

Paperback ISBN: 9781955683838

Ebook ISBN: 9781955683845

Cover Design: Red Thread Designs

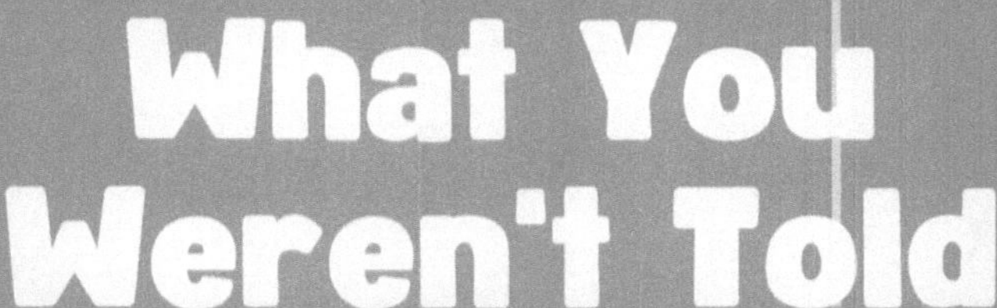

What You Weren't Told

A Parent's Guide
to Raising Kids Who Love to Read

MICHELLE GOMES

For my Family

CONTENTS

INTRODUCTION

Before becoming a nurse, I worked in law enforcement and spent many years in juvenile corrections. I would work with incarcerated youth daily while being a mom to my five-year-old son by night. When it came to reading, I began noticing the connection between what was occurring in our public school system and the juvenile corrections system. The incarcerated youth would technically be in middle and high school grades, yet they were reading at 3rd- and 4th-grade reading levels, and their writing was equally as poor. I couldn't understand how kids could make it to high school barely able to read.

However, as my son grew and moved up in grade, I could see exactly how this could happen. Regardless of how my son struggled with reading or any subject, he moved on to the next stage; so long as he met the bare minimum reading requirements for the school year, he moved on to the next grade.

Teachers and support were available for additional help and support, but it was minimal. They had more students than they had time to give. They were operating with poor and outdated teaching materials; they couldn't deviate from the school department's curriculum even if they were not in agreement with it, and there were times when teaching hardly took place because they tended to behavioral issues within the class. Retaining kids, which means having kids repeat a grade, is an unpopular solution amongst teachers and parents, so kids, even when they aren't performing on the appropriate reading level, get passed on to the next grade. Also, unfavorably, the kids who are kept back tend to be children of African-American, Latin, and Asian backgrounds, and the standardized test used to measure their reading level is also not in their favor.

"Modern critics note that standardized test scores largely reflect socioeconomic privilege. That's partly because rich kids with mediocre scores can juice their results with expensive private test preparation courses. Also, differences in test results among students from different backgrounds may be related to an array of issues from early childhood malnutrition to differences in resources available at local schools."

— (*ANNUAL REVIEW OF SOCIOLOGY, ERIC GRODSKY, JOHN ROBERT WARREN, AND ERIKA FELTS, 2008*).

Thus, year after year, kids in this country are moving up in grade level, all while falling further behind in their reading level.

Does this mean that kids must repeat a grade when they are behind in their reading? No, it does not.

What it means is that the current solutions in schools, like standardized testing and lack of resources, aren't working and, most importantly, out of parents' control. I don't know about you, but I am a parent who is a proponent of focusing on the things I can control and placing my energies there.

Also, the school-to-prison pipeline is accurate, as I witnessed with my work. If I were going to keep my son from becoming an incarcerated youth, my level of involvement in his reading journey needed to increase. As parents, focusing on what we can control looks like continuing to give our input, support, and advocate for our children and change in their schools while simultaneously maintaining the outcome of their reading success at home. According to the National Center for Families Learning,

> "60 percent of parents with children in grades k-8 admit they have trouble helping with their children's homework."

Are you one of the 60 percent?

Admittedly, I once was, especially when helping my son with his reading homework.

HOW I LEARNED TO TEACH MY SON TO READ

Teaching my son to read was a journey, not like those pictures you see on the internet where a person is in a car, bags packed and hanging out the driver's side window, smiling. Our journey had ups and downs; sometimes, we smiled, and other times, we wanted out of the car altogether. Like many parents, I doubted my abilities and wasn't sure if I would succeed, but I knew I had to start. I was a single parent working upwards of 60 hours a week with a small support system, and I felt afraid and overwhelmed. However, my son depended on me for both life and academic skills. In my world, neither of those skill sets was more important than the other, and it was apparent I couldn't leave the responsibility in the hands of others.

I was a college graduate from public- and private-school backgrounds and the child of teenage parents. I came from low- and middle-class socioeconomic environments and lived in the homes to match. Stereotypically, I was the last person who should have the audacity to think I could teach my son. However, drawing on my stereotypical "weaknesses" is what I used to help him.

I was a survivor of adversity, and determined to teach him to be the same. We started with letters and letter sounds. I read to him daily, and he would read to me as he became older. I requested weekly updates on what he was working on at school. If he didn't come home with work, I created my assignment based on their learning in school. We took our time, I made it fun, and when things became tough, we'd do what we could and start again the next day. I gave him what the schools couldn't: one-on-one attention and time, a non-judgemental place to repeat subject matter until he mastered and understood it, an array of updated books we chose together, and applied the lessons to real life.

I taught with love.

Why I Wrote This Book and How It Will Benefit You

My then 5-year-old son is in his twenties, and my family has grown. There is my 6-year-old daughter, Lyric, and my 5-year-old son, Ahmad. When they were toddlers, I was back looking for reading materials. I noticed not much had changed. Parents I spoke with were still frustrated about what their kids were learning and failing to learn at school, and they wanted to help but felt they didn't know how. Having lived this experience with my first son, I was eager to help. I also realized that this problem of parents wanting to help their children learn to read wasn't solely a local issue, but also a global issue.

There are endless amounts of information out there on parenting. This book will shed light on how I've introduced reading into my children's and other children's lives around the globe. For instance, while I've birthed more beautiful babies since that hot day in August, I've also birthed my company, *Levels2learning*, bringing inclusive reading materials to homes and schools, and helping parents learn the best tools for integrating reading into their children's lives no matter what their reading levels and ages are.

I aim to offer this book and my website to increase the number of parents who feel equipped to help their children learn and love to read. This book and my website are grounded in my lived experiences with science-based information added in when necessary; I was once a parent who doubted my ability to teach my child to read and where to start.

Not only did I raise my son to read and read well, but he also enjoys reading. He purchased his bookcase unprompted and the books to put in it. He no longer reads for grades; he reads for leisure and continued growth.

The problem I encountered with many books that claimed to help parents teach their children to read was that they focused on the technical skills of reading, like phonics and blending, and even came with weekly curricula. Even when the writers stated they were parents themselves, I still felt like I was being spoken to as if I were a teacher and not a parent. The writers still wrote as if they were addressing their fellow teachers. The other issue I encountered was the lack of attention those books gave to all the other areas of reading that must be present for a child to learn to read.

These are areas of reading that parents undoubtedly have to offer their children. Teachers help children to read in preparation for the next grade; parents help their children to read in preparation for life.

NOTES:

Key learnings from this chapter

In Utero

It was 2003 and one of the hottest days in August. I was double-parked on a narrow one-way street in Philly, intending to run in and out of my Ob-Gyn appointment. However, the universe had other plans for me. "You're pregnant," my doctor said. As disbelief filled my mind and body, I braced myself for the new adventure unfolding in my life. There's a newfound kind of instinct that happens when you become a mother; mine led me to the bookstore—Barnes and Noble in Center City, to be exact.

For as long as I can remember, bookstores, libraries, and books provided me the space to feel safe, relaxed, and at peace. When I reached the bookstore, I did three things: I grabbed a set of headphones and listened to a CD (we could do that back then), I picked out a couple of books about pregnancy, and I purchased my baby's first book. Maybe I didn't know much about being pregnant or raising a baby, but I did know books. My love of reading was deeply ingrained in who I was and was how I'd found peace and joy in this world, and while I wasn't sure what motherhood would bring for me, I was sure I wanted to share my love of reading.

There are endless amounts of information out there on parenting. Most parenting magazines, reading journals, and milestone charts tell us that reading to our children begins at age 2. At the same time, others encourage parents to start reading during pregnancy. I prefer the latter. A few essential things occur when we read to our babies when pregnant. Our babies become familiar with the sound of our voice; we bond with them, and it promotes brain development. So, at what stage of pregnancy do we begin reading to our growing baby?

According to science, we can start reading to our babies in the sixth month of pregnancy. By the sixth month, babies in utero can hear sounds clearly. So, how do we read to our baby-to-be?

Most importantly, how do we read to them in a way that doesn't feel silly or like we're talking to ourselves? Both are good questions and legitimate concerns for expectant parents. I, too, felt a bit silly at first, but as with anything new to us, the more we do it, the better we get.

No matter when you start reading, five key factors support a healthy reading environment.

KEY FACTOR #1: SELECTING THE RIGHT BOOKS

Honestly, there is no right or wrong here. You want to pick a book that resonates with you and that you'd enjoy reading to your child pre- and post-birth. I teach parents to start with a board book in my homeschooling programs. Board books are short, sturdy, and geared toward the baby age group. These are easy for babies to hold and feel during reading, appealing to their curiosity and senses. You'll want to continue sharing the book with your baby once he or she arrives. Start with five to ten minutes because your free time and baby's attention will initially be limited.

Also, do not become preoccupied with the book learning

content yet. By all means, feel free to pick a book about ABCs or colors, but be sure to include silly rhyming books that are fun and engaging. Keep these books in your chosen reading space and make it an exciting time to spend together from day one. This will help to teach your child as they grow up that this is a unique space and create the idea that reading is what we do here.

Key Factor #2: For Expecting Mamas

Pregnancy is magical and scary for many expecting parents. It's essential to take time before the baby arrives to consider how you want to include reading into your routine. If you wish to utilize your reading space or relax on the couch or in bed, this can be a time for partners to bond and connect.

Consider how you want to incorporate yourself and your partner into your reading area. Do this when you are most relaxed. I firmly believe that when stressed as pregnant women, our babies and bodies feel every bit of our stress. We need to be mindful of how we set the tone for reading to our baby. Now that we are relaxed and ready to be in tune with our baby and bodies, we set the atmosphere.

Considering that we are reading to our womb, I encourage

you to select an area quiet enough to hear a pin drop, as the saying goes. For example, my go-to space was my bedroom. There were no distractions, and I found my bed comforting. Once you have created your quiet place, try to keep it free of all distractions—your cell and television must be off and out of reach. Make sure you have comfortable seating or a place to lay. Place a comfortable pillow behind you and underneath your feet. Next, position yourself so your head and voice are toward your baby.

With your book of choice, begin reading the book as you would if your baby were in your arms. You do not need to scream the words from the book, but I suggest speaking up. While reading, feel free to improvise on the story, use emotion in your voice and take the time to touch your belly before, during, and after.

Do not underestimate the power of incorporating touch. Touch is equally as crucial in this process as your voice. Also, this is a great time to include your favorite massage oils. Our voices, human touch, and closeness convey positive emotions to our children before and after arrival; for those uncomfortable with contact to express love or positive feelings but who want to be able to do so with their child, this is a great place to start. You can practice without judgment and make it your own.

KEY FACTOR #3: INCLUDE FAMILY

Yes, that's right, reading to your baby bump can be a great way to get your baby attuned to other critical family voices, stimulate your baby's brain, and allow others to bond with them (MamaFIT UK 2022). Designate one person at a time, following the same steps. Set boundaries if you are uncomfortable with others touching your baby bump and only want them to share in the reading. This is not meant to be stressful, but rather a relaxing and fun activity. You can invite siblings as well; they can simply talk to the baby about something fun, make up their own story or sing a nursery rhyme. The sky's the limit.

KEY FACTOR #4: BABY REGISTRIES

When I review baby registries, the first thing I look for is books. Guess what? There are few, if any, listed. I understand that when we, as parents, create our registries, we are focused on the most essential and urgently needed items. However, given the increasing illiteracy in our country, I'd argue that having books on our baby registries is crucial and urgent.

When our babies are out of diapers, have outgrown all the toys, and no longer need car seats or strollers, their books and their literacy will remain necessities. A great way to make your reading nook special is to invite baby shower guests to replace giving cards with books with a personalized message they can give to your upcoming bundle of joy. Guests can also pass down a book they already have from their kids to keep them in circulation.

KEY FACTOR #5: THE ENVIRONMENT

You know the saying "Out of sight, out of mind?" The same goes for children and books. To cultivate a love of reading, children must visually see books in their home environment. When the only access and interaction they have with books is in school or for homework, that is what they come to associate reading and books with. As parents, it is our responsibility to show our children that books are not only academic tools, but are also for enjoyment, personal growth, adventure, connection, and even healing.

Creating the right environment for reading can look and feel like anything you want. Consider your personality: what you want your baby to touch and envision for themselves daily as they grow in this nursery, and what feels fun, creative, or peaceful for you. Select simple and safe decor to make it a special place. Some things some of my clients have done to make their reading space unique include the following:

- adding a bookshelf or book basket
- hanging a poster of the alphabet
- including storybook puppets with their toys

As your child grows, consider organizing the books so that the book covers are front-facing, rather than by their book spines; this will spark your child's interest and curiosity in them. Also, placing the books at a reachable level will promote your child's independence in reading.

NOTES:

Key learnings from this chapter

BUILDING A READING FOUNDATION

A child's reading foundation looks something like this: the letters of the alphabet, letter sounds, blending, word identification, and then using these collectively to read. When our children are infants and toddlers, we start them off with learning the letters of the alphabet. We purchase everything from alphabet blocks to those fancy baby wall borders with the ABCs imprinted on them. As they grow and make their way into preschool, they begin learning the sounds that each letter of the alphabet makes, how those sounds come together to make words (also known as blending), and how that creates the sentences in the books they read. There are words you will hear at this stage that will be helpful to you; their definitions are as follows:

- **Phonics**: A method of teaching reading by using letters and their matching sounds
- **Phonemes**: The smallest units of sounds, in English, that distinguish one word from another. There are forty-four of them. For example, the difference between the words "cat" and "hat" is

the beginning sound— the phoneme—that starts each word.

- **Blending**: Joining speech sounds to make a word
- **Decoding**: The skill of taking a written word and knowing the sounds that each letter makes to translate it into a spoken word. This is sometimes referred to as "sounding out" a word.

Now that we have addressed the technicalities of reading and their relevance to your child's reading foundation, let's discuss them beyond their definitions and not-so-technical aspects that impact a child's reading foundation.

Not all children learn through the sole use of phonics. You can teach letters, letter sounds, and words; however, each child is different. Some children may do well with phonics instruction only while others may need a combination of methods. It is important for parents to understand this because if your child's school has a curriculum with a strict focus on phonics and your child is still struggling to read, you will have to incorporate other strategies at home to help your child learn to read. You'll also want to inquire about what the plan is should your child begin to fall behind in the chosen reading instruction. Will you be notified immediately? What interventions will the school and teacher put in place to ensure your child is caught up by the end of the school year? When homeschooling, take advantage of having the flexibility to utilize any combination of reading methods necessary to help your child learn to read.

Telling Your Child to "Sound the Words Out" Will Only Take Them so Far

This is because letters can have different sounds depending on the word they are in; how a letter may sound in one word may not be true for its sound in the next.

Utilize Alphabet Charts Wisely

Children can know the letters by the order in which they learn to recite them; however, that isn't always an indication that they know them well. Try teaching them in a different order at times to give your children the opportunity to get familiar with identifying the letters in random order. Also have them practice in real-world environments, identifying letters on street signs, food products, and anywhere in the home where letters can be found. Last, some of the images used in the alphabet chart and their accompanying words can be difficult for beginner learners, particularly toddlers. When selecting alphabet charts, consider the ones with the letters only.

Start With the Letters and Sounds that are the Easiest for Young Children to Pronounce

Depending on their ages and abilities, some children may not be able to pronounce all letter sounds. If your child has speech delay or is struggling with a letter, move on to the next one and revisit the more challenging letter sounds later. My Levels2learning website has resources detailing the letter sounds best suited for specific ages.

USE GAMES TO TEACH THE LETTERS AND SOUNDS

Scavenger hunts, letter bingo, Play-doh, and paint are great ways to make letter learning engaging. Once your child is familiar with the letters and sounds try practicing without the "sight" piece. For instance, say the sound and ask them to tell you its corresponding letter, or vice versa.

DON'T LIMIT YOUR CHILD'S LEARNING

You can practice more than one letter at a time. Introduce two letters first; if they are learning quickly, add a third. If they are doing well with one letter at a time, continue with that. Remember: quality over quantity. The same goes for introducing words: you do not have to start with three-letter words. Instead begin with two-letter words such as "up" and "on." Another approach is beginning with one-syllable words then progressing to two and three syllables. Teach your child to identify the syllables to words using the clapping method. A word that can be stated within one clap—such as "dog"— is a one-syllable word. Two-syllable words would be "apple" and so forth.

CHOOSING WORDS TO START WITH

When choosing words to start with, we are most often told to refer to both "Dolch" and "Frye" lists, which are used in schools. These lists consist of suggested vocabulary words for pre-k to third grade students and are most commonly referred to as "sight words." However, there is a third list referred to as the "functional" word list. Functional words are good to start with, particularly for toddlers, because they are usually the words that help children get their needs met. Most functional words are verbs such as "run," "eat," and "stop." Refer to the links below for the functional word list method. https://levels2learning.com/

CREATING BEGINNER SENTENCES

Select three to five words from the lists provided to create a beginner sentence. For example, "The dog likes to run." By creating and practicing sentences such as these, you're teaching your child their first vocabulary words, sentence structure, and reading.

NOTES:

Key learnings from this chapter

MEET THEM WHERE
THEY ARE

As a parent, I do my best to visit my kids' classrooms when there are kids present and class is in session, even more so when a "problem" arises. My daughter's first year of kindergarten was far from what I had anticipated. It was one challenge after another. However, whenever I asked for answers, the teachers seemed only to remember the aftermath, the negative. As a parent, I didn't find that to be helpful. I needed to know what led up to the incidents my daughter was having so that we could come up with proactive, rather than reactive solutions. In response, I was granted permission to observe her class. When I walked in first thing in the morning, I noticed children divided into groups, sitting perhaps six at a semi-circle table, working on their writing. Overall it didn't *feel* like I was observing 5-year-olds; it *felt* more like a college lecture hall setting. If there was play incorporated into the class, it wasn't apparent. I looked around for signs of sensory play items and toys that could be simultaneously used for play and teaching—things they could touch, feel, smell, or listen to so they could make sense of what they were learning. I noticed none. At this age, kids have just transitioned from home care or daycare settings. They were in environments where they were learning through play that engaged all five of their senses. They were spending their days where naps were allowed, they could move their bodies about, and being social was the norm. Toys, used for play and learning, were within reach, they were exposed to the outdoors more than once a day, and social-emotional learning was as much a part of their day as their reading, writing, and math. Fast forward to kindergarten, and suddenly, naptime is gone, toys are nowhere to be found, and recess is once a day for a few minutes. As for social-emotional learning, it's not a part of the curriculum. We have 5-year-olds who are expected to sit for long hours without talking or moving so that they can complete tedious and redundant black-and-white dittos. Worse, if your kid doesn't fit into this mold, they are labeled and treated as a "problem."

Subsequently, after dealing with a racist principal, a school system that still condoned suspending 5-year-olds and having the police called to escort her from the building, Lyric was transferred to a "more restrictive setting." Do you know what I found? Everything I wanted for my daughter. The classroom was small in size, with no more than six kids. It was stuffed wall-to-wall with toys for both academic and social-emotional learning. There was a cozy book nook filled with books, bean bags, and a rug. The children had room to spread out, headphones hung up for listening to lessons, and even a mini-garden. Play-doh was accessible for math and letter learning, and their outdoor playground still had a structured playset. Her new kindergarten classroom, teacher, and learning materials were all the things every kindergarten student should have access to. Her new learning environment made room for what the previous one lacked: an openness to the different ways in which each child learns.

One of the most common mistakes is not teaching

children to read using different learning styles. Some parents automatically teach their children the same way the teachers in school teach them, others use techniques that worked for them growing up, and the remaining parents don't know that different learning styles exist. The problem is that children are individuals and do not learn in a "one-style-fits-all" manner. Chances are your child's learning style falls into one of the following four categories: Visual, Aural, Verbal, or Physical.

Visual learning involves observation, pictures, graphs, and whiteboards. Visual learners must see the information presented to them to grasp it. Aural learners learn best when they can listen to the learning material; examples of this are people who listen to speeches, audiobooks, and recordings to comprehend what is taught. Next are the verbal learners; these children learn best through discussing the material. When introduced, they do best by talking the lesson over with someone to understand it better: think of study groups or kids reviewing flashcards while whispering to themselves. For younger children, an example would be having them read aloud or talk about the pictures on a page when learning to read. Last is the physical. Physical learners get the most out of learning by using their bodies, movement, and touch to understand their learning. These are your kids who learn well when learning games are brought out, when they are asked to build or construct a project, and perhaps even bake. These kids get the most out of learning when it is physically interactive.

So how do we, as parents, determine which learning style is best to use when teaching our children? Observation and interaction. If you want to know how your child learns best, you must watch them while working with them. More importantly, it will take consistently showing up to work with them to understand what style or styles work for them. One way to do this is to select a topic; for instance, let's use the example of the ocean and different types of sea animals for our early learners.

VISUAL LEARNING:

Visual learners thrive when they can see and process information through images and diagrams. Start by gathering colorful pictures of the ocean, vibrant fish, and other marine creatures. These images should be captivating and detailed, sparking curiosity and wonder. As you share these images with your child, encourage them to describe what they see, ask questions, and express their thoughts. This verbal interaction will reinforce their understanding and retention of the visuals. Engage their imagination by encouraging them to imagine themselves diving into the ocean and exploring its mysteries.

VERBAL LEARNING:

Engaging in meaningful conversations and discussions is critical for verbal learners. Use the pictures as prompts for conversation. Discuss with your child the different types of fish, their colors, sizes, and habitats. Share interesting facts and anecdotes related to the ocean and marine life. Encourage your child to ask questions and express their thoughts as well. This verbal exchange will enhance their understanding and develop their language skills. Consider incorporating storytelling, where you create a narrative around a fish's journey through the ocean, making it both educational and entertaining.

AURAL LEARNING:

Aural learners absorb information best through hearing and listening. Introduce them to children's audiobooks or television programs on ocean exploration and marine biology. Channels like PBS or National Geographic Kids often provide engaging content that presents facts and stories through captivating narrations. This allows your child to make connections and learn through auditory experiences. Encourage them to discuss what they've heard and share their favorite parts.

PHYSICAL LEARNING:

For those who learn best through physical engagement, use toys that feature fish and marine creatures to facilitate learning. Use your collected pictures to play games like mix-and-match, memory, or scavenger hunts. This approach combines visual engagement with tactile interaction, making the learning experience more immersive and memorable. You can even create simple craft activities where your child constructs their own fish or ocean scene using paper, clay, or other materials.

Incorporating these different learning styles makes a holistic and engaging learning journey for your child. Remember that children often have a dominant learning style but can benefit from exposure to other methods, enhancing their overall learning experience and making it enjoyable and effective.

Notes:

Key learnings from this chapter

"MIRRORS AND WINDOWS"

Growing up, I read many books that did not have characters who looked like me, nor were their lives anything like mine. Most books displayed at the bookstore and library were of young Caucasian kids. In school, it was more of the same. It wasn't until middle school that I was finally exposed to books with African-American main characters.

Integrating these books into my reading curriculum forever improved my reading experience. For instance, when reading books such as *Sweet Valley High* or *The Babysitters Club*, I read them as an excited, nosey outsider looking in. It was as if I were a classmate or neighbor to the kids I was reading about. I understood the stories and enjoyed them, but there was a disconnect. I almost always pictured the girls according to societal standards: blue eyes, blonde hair, and pretty unless the author depicted otherwise.

On the other hand, when reading *Roll of Thunder, Hear My Cry* and *The Bluest Eye*, I became immersed in the characters' stories. The Black girls in those stories were me, and I was them. Their families, thoughts, and some of their experiences were relatable. Gone were the days of being an outsider; I could now picture myself in the stories. From that moment on, armed with my new awareness of books that existed with characters and stories that I could relate to, I read more and naturally enjoyed it more. I no longer had to feel disconnected from the stories I read. I no longer had to sit in classrooms and continue to go through life feeling like books weren't intended for kids who looked like me or written for little black girls and boys to enjoy.

As a parent, I later learned that there was a term to explain what I was experiencing. The term is "mirrors and windows." The concept of "mirrors and windows" in reading, which refers to the idea that literature can serve as both a mirror reflecting a reader's own experiences and a window into the experiences of others, was popularized by Dr. Rudine Sims Bishop. Dr. Bishop is a renowned scholar and educator in the field of children's literature, particularly in the context of diversity and multiculturalism.

"Mirror" books have characters with the same race, culture and gender as the reader. "Window" books have characters differing in race, culture, and gender from the reader. To be successful readers, children need both mirror and window books. Mirror books are necessary for children to gain a healthy knowledge and acceptance of themselves, their race, culture, religions, families, lived experiences, and where they fit within their communities. Window books help create well-rounded readers, giving them an inside look and increasing their knowledge and understanding of others who are different from them.

In a world rich with diverse cultures, languages, and experiences, teaching your children to read goes beyond the words on the page. It's an opportunity to open their minds, broaden their horizons, and nurture their understanding and appreciation of the world's diverse tapestry. Incorporating diversity, culture, and inclusion into your reading journey not only enriches their education but also helps them become compassionate, empathetic individuals. Here's how you can create an inclusive reading environment, utilizing both "mirror and window" books, that celebrates the beauty of our global community.

DIVERSE BOOK SELECTION:

Start by curating a collection of books that reflects a wide range of cultures, backgrounds, and perspectives. Seek out stories that feature characters from various ethnicities, religions, abilities, and socio-economic backgrounds. When children see themselves represented in the stories they read, it fosters a sense of belonging and validation. Moreover, exposure to diverse characters helps break down stereotypes and promotes empathy. Consider the book's storyline. Is it relatable? Is it something your children can connect with, understand, and apply to their inner and outer worlds?

EXPLORE NEW WORLDS:

Use literature as a bridge to new cultures and experiences. Select books that transport your children to different countries, traditions, and historical periods. Before reading, take a moment to research and discuss the cultural context. This enhances their understanding and allows them to engage with the story on a deeper level. Encourage questions and conversations about the similarities and differences between their own lives and the lives of the characters they're reading about.

Multilingual Exploration:

If your family speaks more than one language, consider incorporating books in those languages into your reading routine. This not only supports language development but also provides insights into the cultural nuances and expressions that might not directly translate into English. Even if you're monolingual, exploring books in other languages can still be a fascinating way to learn about different cultures.

Discuss Diversity:

Encourage open discussions about diversity, inclusion, and cultural differences as you read together. Ask questions that prompt your children to think critically about the themes in the story. Explore topics like identity, prejudice, and social justice. These conversations help them develop a nuanced understanding of the world around them and become allies for equity and justice.

Author and Illustrator Diversity:

In the intricate fabric of literature, authors and illustrators are the weavers who bring stories to life, infusing them with their unique backgrounds, experiences, and viewpoints. Recognizing and embracing this diversity in the creators behind the books is a powerful way to foster a richer and more authentic reading experience for your children. Here's why author and illustrator diversity matters, and how you can weave it seamlessly into your reading journey.

BROADENING HORIZONS:

Just as the world is a tapestry of cultures, so, too, is the literary landscape. Diverse authors and illustrators contribute their individual perspectives, cultural insights, and personal stories to the stories they craft. By seeking out these creators, you open doors to new worlds, perspectives, and narratives that might not otherwise find their way onto your bookshelf. Your children are exposed to a broader range of experiences, sparking curiosity and expanding their understanding of the human experience.

AUTHENTIC AND NUANCED STORIES:

Authenticity matters in storytelling. When authors and illustrators draw from their own cultural backgrounds and personal journeys, their stories resonate more deeply with readers. The nuances, emotions, and details they infuse into their work create a level of authenticity that connects readers to characters and situations in meaningful ways. By exploring stories from diverse creators, your children gain insights into cultures, traditions, and realities that may differ from their own, fostering empathy and understanding.

CULTIVATING IDENTITY AND REPRESENTATION:

Children are constantly forming their sense of identity and their place in the world. Seeing authors and illustrators who share their backgrounds or experiences provides them with role models and validates their identities. It sends a powerful message that their stories and perspectives matter, fostering a sense of pride and empowerment. For children from marginalized backgrounds, representation in literature helps combat feelings of isolation and invisibility.

Critical Thinking and Empathy:

Engaging with stories from diverse creators encourages critical thinking. Your children learn to question assumptions, challenge stereotypes, and consider alternative viewpoints. These skills are vital for developing open-mindedness and empathy, enabling them to navigate a multicultural world with respect and understanding.

Cultivating Curiosity:

The process of exploring diverse authors and illustrators can be an adventure in itself. Together with your children, you can embark on a journey to discover new voices, research cultural contexts, and delve into the personal stories of the creators. This exploration nurtures curiosity, as you learn about the authors' inspirations, challenges, and motivations behind their works.

Creating Future Advocates:

Reading books by diverse authors and illustrators lays the foundation for your children to become advocates for inclusivity and equality. They learn that literature is a powerful tool for amplifying marginalized voices and challenging the status quo. This awareness can inspire them to stand up against injustice, amplify diverse perspectives, and create a more inclusive world.

As you embark on your reading journey, make it a delightful exploration of both stories and the minds that create them. By actively seeking out diverse authors and illustrators, you're nurturing a love for literature that transcends cultural boundaries and fosters a deep appreciation for the myriad of stories that weave our world together.

Once you have created an inclusive reading environment by using the ideas listed previously and purposely decided on the books and stories that utilize the mirror and windows theory, take the exploration and learning off the pages and into activities that help solidify learning for children. By incorporating the following activities you will be able to reinforce what you and your child have read, creating an even more inclusive perspective.

Cultural Activities:

Stories have the incredible power to transport us to new worlds, allowing us to experience different cultures, traditions, and ways of life. But what if you could take that experience a step further? Cultural activities provide a tangible connection to the stories your children read, offering them an immersive and engaging way to explore diverse cultures. By extending the reading experience with hands-on activities, you're creating a dynamic and holistic learning journey that enhances your children's cultural understanding in unforgettable ways.

COOKING ADVENTURES:

Food is a universal language that transcends borders and brings people together. If a story features a traditional dish or culinary tradition, why not embark on a cooking adventure? Research recipes that align with the story's cultural context and cook the dish together as a family. As you chop, stir, and savor the flavors, you're not only creating a delicious meal, but also building a deeper connection to the story's setting and characters.

CRAFTS AND TRADITIONS:

Many stories showcase unique crafts, traditions, and celebrations that are an integral part of a culture. Explore these aspects further by engaging in related craft activities. Whether it's creating paper lanterns for a lantern festival, making colorful masks for a carnival, or crafting origami inspired by Japanese tales, these hands-on projects allow your children to experience cultural elements firsthand.

INTERACTIVE EXPLORATION:

Turn your home into a mini-museum by setting up interactive displays that reflect the cultural elements in the stories you've read. For instance, if a story is set in ancient Egypt, create a mini Egyptian exhibit complete with hieroglyphic writing, artifacts, and images of pyramids. This immersive environment encourages your children to delve deeper into the story's context and engage with the culture in a dynamic way.

Music and Dance:

Music and dance are integral components of many cultures. If a story features traditional songs or dances, explore these artistic expressions with your children. Listen to music from the story's region, learn simple dance steps, or even create your own music-inspired crafts, like making musical instruments from recycled materials.

Cultural Festivals and Celebrations:

Research cultural festivals, holidays, and celebrations related to the stories you've read. Participate in local events or create your own celebrations at home. Whether it's a Lunar New Year feast, a Diwali-inspired light display, or a Day of the Dead altar, these activities provide insights into cultural traditions and celebrations.

Virtual Field Trips:

If physical travel isn't an option, consider embarking on virtual field trips to explore the cultures depicted in the stories. Use online resources to virtually tour museums, historical sites, and cultural landmarks from around the world. This virtual exploration enriches your children's understanding of the story's setting and context.

By actively participating in cultural events and engaging with your local community, you create invaluable opportunities for your children to witness diversity in action. These real-world interactions reinforce the invaluable lessons they've absorbed from books and empower them to wholeheartedly embrace inclusivity and respect for all. These experiences ultimately bond your family with a broader global community, where you collectively celebrate the profound beauty of human differences and unite in a shared appreciation for the rich mosaic of cultures that enrich our world.

As you seamlessly integrate diversity, culture, and inclusion into your children's reading journey, you're not merely fostering their literacy skills; you're also nurturing their awareness of the kaleidoscope of perspectives that shape our world. Through these inclusive experiences, you are helping your children evolve into global citizens who ardently champion differences, advocate for equality, and make positive contributions to the diverse communities they are an integral part of.

NOTES:

Key learnings from this chapter

YOUR READING
VILLAGE

As I was growing up, my family was extremely supportive and contributed what they could to my education. It was my grandmother taking us to the libraries and bookstores on the weekends. My dad had the uncomfortable but necessary conversations with us about the consequences of being illiterate and uneducated youth-turned-adults in today's society. It was my uncles and aunts who were good at math and willing to help me during their free time. It was my mom reading us bedtime stories, spending late nights at the dinner table doing our homework with us until we understood it. It was teachers staying after class with me and college students helping as part of their work-study requirements. It was my sister who looked to me for guidance on the cool books to read, so I needed to keep going because if I stopped then she'd stop. When I became a mom, I already knew raising a reader wasn't a solo journey.

However, I was living out-of-state at the time and what I had come to know as my reading village was miles away. So I did what I could and worked with what I had. I could make it to the local libraries and bookstores with my son. His father and I both loved to read, so we read to him, and later with him. I enrolled him in a daycare with caregivers who valued early childhood education. The friends I made as well as their parents who babysat read to him. When we moved back home, what was once my reading village was now my son's.

In a world where strong family support might not always be readily available, creating a nurturing reading environment for your children can seem daunting. However, the absence of immediate family doesn't mean you can't build your reading village, a community of support that encourages and fosters a love for books and learning in your children. With determination, creativity, and extra effort, you can cultivate a thriving reading village to enrich your child's literary journey. I've crafted some great suggestions for you below.

EMBRACE THE POWER OF FRIENDS

While traditional family support can be invaluable, close friends who share similar values and interests can become integral members of your reading village. Seek friends who prioritize reading and learning, collaborate to exchange book recommendations, organize reading playdates, and host mini-book clubs. You can establish a support network beyond blood ties by forging strong connections with these like-minded individuals.

CONNECT WITH COMMUNITY RESOURCES

Communities often have resources that can be pivotal in your child's reading journey. Public libraries, for instance, offer a treasure trove of books and host various reading-related events. Regular library visits can introduce your child to the joy of discovering new stories while connecting with other young readers. Many libraries also organize reading challenges, workshops, and storytelling sessions that can further engage your child's interest in books. Mentoring programs and sorority and fraternity community reading events are also options.

LEVERAGE ONLINE COMMUNITIES

In today's digital age, the lack of traditional family support doesn't have to be a barrier. Online communities and platforms can provide access to a global network of parents and caregivers passionate about nurturing young readers. Join social media groups, forums, and websites dedicated to children's literature and parenting. Participate in virtual book clubs, discussions, and even online reading sessions to ensure your child has exposure to diverse reading experiences.

COLLABORATE WITH TEACHERS AND EDUCATORS

Schools and educational institutions are natural partners in your endeavor to create a reading village. Regularly communicate with your child's teachers to understand their reading curriculum and recommended books. Engage in conversations about your child's reading habits and seek advice on fostering a love for books at home. Many schools also host literacy events, book fairs, and reading challenges that you can actively participate in. Seek out a storyteller for their birthday parties.

HOST YOUR OWN READING EVENTS

Turn your home into a hub of reading activity by hosting your own reading events. Invite neighbors, friends, and classmates for themed reading parties, storytelling nights, or book-exchange gatherings.

VOLUNTEER AND COLLABORATE

Engage in community volunteering or collaboration with local organizations that promote literacy. Participating in initiatives such as book drives, reading workshops, or mentoring programs not only contributes to your child's reading village, but it also exposes them to the value of giving back and sharing knowledge.

BE AN ACTIVE READING ROLE MODEL

Your enthusiasm for reading can profoundly impact your child. Model a love for books by incorporating reading into your daily routine. Let your child see you reading various materials, from novels to magazines. Engage in discussions about what you're reading, and encourage your child to do the same. By displaying your genuine interest in reading, you can inspire them to develop their own passion for books.

Building a reading village is about creating a supportive environment that fosters a love for books and learning, regardless of traditional family support. By tapping into friendships, community resources, online platforms, and your dedication, you can shape a rich reading life for your child that will stay with them.

NOTES:

Key learnings from this chapter

PUT YOURSELF IN THEIR SHOES

Maria was a young Mexican-American co-worker of mine, somewhere in her twenties. One day we were discussing our families and she mentioned that she was the youngest of ten children in a single-parent household. Being intrigued, I asked her how she learned to read in such a large family. She explained that whenever it was time to read or do any kind of homework, she and her siblings were called to do it in the family dining room. When they refused to do their reading or attempted to get out of it, their mother would threaten to hit them with her slipper and impose other punishments, none of which led to change. In fact, Maria confessed that she and her siblings would pretend to read or read just enough to answer questions and get passing grades. As Maria and her siblings grew older the consequences were even less effective. All the slippers and punishments did was increase her dislike for reading and, once out of school, she never picked up a book again. When I asked her what she would do differently when she has children of her own, she responded with "I don't know, but it won't be the slipper."

As we've already discovered, we often find ourselves taking the lead role in our children's learning journey. Just as we hold their tiny hands as they take their first steps, we also hold their hands as they venture into the magical realm of books. But perhaps one of the most beautiful aspects of this journey is meeting our children exactly where they are in their reading process.

Pushing a child too hard in the reading process can inadvertently create a rift between them and the world of books. While the intention might be to accelerate their learning, the consequences can be counterproductive and emotionally taxing. When children are pushed beyond their comfort zones and developmental readiness, several negative outcomes can emerge.

Firstly, excessive pressure can lead to a sense of inadequacy and self-doubt. Children may start believing that their worth is solely determined by their reading abilities, which can erode their self-esteem. Instead of experiencing the joy of reading, they may associate it with stress and performance anxiety.

Additionally, pushing a child too hard can foster a disinterest in reading altogether. When the focus shifts from the delight of storytelling to the pressure of reaching arbitrary milestones, children may begin to see reading as a chore rather than a pleasurable activity. This can lead to avoidance behaviors and reluctance to engage with books, stunting their overall growth as readers.

Furthermore, pushing a child beyond their readiness can hinder their comprehension and critical-thinking skills. When they're forced to tackle texts that are too complex for their cognitive level, they may struggle to understand and retain the material. This can create gaps in their understanding, making it difficult for them to connect with more appropriate reading materials in the future.

Ultimately, pushing a child too hard in the reading process

can strain the parent-child relationship. Instead of being a source of comfort and support, reading time can become a battleground of frustration and tension. Children might perceive their parents as being more focused on their achievements than on their well-being and happiness.

In fostering a lifelong love for reading, it's essential to remember that every child has their own pace of development. Respect for their individuality and readiness is key. By creating a nurturing and relaxed environment where reading is cherished, children are more likely to naturally progress and flourish on their reading journeys.

You can easily do this by setting reading goals together. Reading isn't a race, it's a voyage of discovery. Just as we wouldn't rush through a breathtaking landscape, we shouldn't rush our children through books. Instead of imposing reading goals upon them, involve your child in the process. Sit down and have a chat about what interests them, what genres they're curious about, and how they feel about their reading skills. Let them have a say in what books they want to explore next. This not only empowers them to take ownership of their reading journey, but it also helps them set achievable goals that ignite their passion.

Another key thing to think about is what your reading journey was as a child. Did you like the way the adults around you supported your reading? What felt good and what didn't? As parents, it's easy to get caught up in ensuring our children are making progress. However, taking a moment to reflect on your own reading journey can be enlightening. Think back to the books that captivated you as a child, the ones that made you fall in love with reading. Recall the times when you got lost in stories, and how those experiences shaped your imagination and worldview. These personal memories can serve as a gentle reminder that reading is more than just a skill; it's a gateway to emotions, adventures, and growth.

Just as every child grows at their own pace physically, they do so mentally as well. Each reading journey is unique, and what matters most is the connection formed, the joy shared, and the love for learning that blossoms. So, when you sit down with your child during those quiet reading times, remember that you're not just guiding them through words on a page. You're fostering a love for reading that will stay with them for a lifetime.

Notes:

Key learnings from this chapter

Kicking The
Boredom Bucket

When my oldest son was in third grade, we were at a reading standoff. He wasn't enjoying reading, and no matter what I did, he didn't want anything to do with it. I was baffled and felt defeated. Until then, I had done everything to ensure he'd embrace books and enjoy reading.

- Read to him pre-birth? *Check!*
- Read to him as an infant and through toddlerhood? *Check!*
- Made reading time fun and exciting? *Check!*

So how did I still end up with a 9-year-old who hated to read? I'll tell you how: mom guilt, ego, and closed-mindedness. I spent so much time—wasted time—concerning myself with where I went wrong and continuing to push upon him traditional reading strategies and rules that I lost sight of the fact that I was raising an ever-changing *individual* in changing times. It is easier for us as parents to continue with what we know, how we were raised, and "tradition" because that's our comfort zone. What's not so easy is change, adapting, and opening up. Sometimes, teaching our kids comes down to being human, being vulnerable, having the confidence to know what isn't working for them or us, and having the courage to make the necessary changes. Just because someone always taught something a certain way doesn't necessarily make it right. Even more importantly, it could be right but not right for you and your child.

So what do we do when encountering a young reader who has long since lost interest? Do we continue to fuss, argue, punish, and lose our cool? Or do we take a calmer approach and release what was so that we can accept what can be? Let's go with the latter and back to our can't-be-bothered reader for argument's sake. I decided to go with my son to the children's section of the bookstore and lead the way. I was mortified by what he picked up, but I didn't verbalize it. Remember, we're keeping an open mind. My son proudly picked up *Captain Underpants*, *Diary of a Wimpy Kid*, and a superhero comic book with illustrations on every page. I could have commented about a kid sticking his butt out on a book cover and a comic book not being "real" reading, but then I reminded myself this wasn't about me; it was about him. Not to mention, what I was doing was no longer working, so it was at this moment that I relinquished my narrowing thoughts and ego and confidently walked with my now-smiling son to the check-out and purchased all three of those books.

Boredom was settling in, and before it was too late I decided it was time to kick the "boredom bucket" and infuse new life into our reading routine.

ENGAGING THE FIVE SENSES:

As the saying goes, "Reading is to the mind what exercise is to the body." But just as physical exercise can become monotonous, so can reading. As I mentioned earlier, encourage your children to engage their five senses while reading. Bring the story to life by incorporating sensory elements. If the characters are savoring a delicious meal, prepare a snack that aligns with the story's cuisine. Is the story about camping or robots? Use items in your house to create an indoor campout or robot. By involving the senses, you're turning a passive reading experience into an interactive adventure.

READING ON THE GO:

Who said reading must be confined to your home's four walls? Turn traveling into a reading adventure. Whether you're on a road trip or waiting at the airport, books can be fantastic companions. Pack a selection of books that cater to different reading preferences and ages. As you journey to new places, the stories can parallel your experiences, enhancing the connection between the fictional world and the real one. Plus, what better way to pass the time during a long journey than immersing yourself in captivating tales?

FLEXIBLE READING TIME:

Life rarely adheres to a perfectly scheduled routine, especially when children are involved. There will be days when your designated reading time clashes with unexpected events. Instead of letting frustration take over, embrace flexibility. Remember that the goal isn't just to check off a reading session, but to create meaningful moments. If the evening reading slot isn't feasible, seize another moment during the day—a lazy morning, a family lunch, or even a cozy bedtime story.

INTERACTIVE STORYTELLING:

Interactive storytelling is a magical way to make reading with your children an engaging and unforgettable experience. It takes reading a step further, turning it into a dynamic adventure where both you and your kids actively participate in shaping the story. This kind of storytelling sparks creativity, boosts critical thinking, and brings you all closer to the heart of the tale.

With interactive storytelling, the lines between the storyteller (that's you!) and the audience (your children) start to blur in the best way possible. Instead of just reading the words on the page, you get to involve your children in creating the story together. You can ask them what they think might happen next, let them invent new characters or twists, and encourage them to express their thoughts. This approach gives your children a sense of control over the story and makes them feel like they're part of the adventure.

Interactive storytelling isn't limited to books alone; you can use this approach with any kind of storytelling medium. Whether you're reading a physical book, sharing an oral story, or even exploring digital stories, the interactive element remains just as powerful. It's an incredible tool for family bonding, nurturing their creativity, and having meaningful conversations.

This method adapts beautifully as your children grow. From their early years when they're excited to share their ideas, to their later years when they're ready to explore more complex narratives and themes, interactive storytelling evolves with them. As parents, you're providing them with a safe space to express themselves, collaborate with you, and develop essential communication skills.

In the end, interactive storytelling transforms reading time into a vibrant journey that both you and your children will cherish. It nurtures their imagination, fosters stronger connections, and ensures that reading is a joyous activity filled with shared moments. Whether you're sitting on a couch or snuggled up in bed, interactive storytelling lets you dive into the wonderful world of stories together.

BOOK EXPLORATION:

I've touched on this before, but as a reminder, sometimes the allure of a new book can work wonders. Take your children to the local library or bookstore and let them explore. Allow them to choose books that resonate with their interests, even if they differ from your own. This empowers them to take ownership of their reading journey, sparking genuine excitement.

As parents, fostering a deeper sense of book exploration with your children is a wonderful way to ignite their curiosity and passion for reading. Beyond the words on the page, there's a whole world of discovery waiting to be uncovered. By engaging in creative activities that support their reading journey, you're not only enhancing their understanding of stories but also building a lifelong love for learning.

CHARACTER ADVENTURES:

Take a step further into the stories by creating character adventures. After reading a book, encourage your children to imagine what might happen next in the lives of their favorite characters. They could draw pictures, write short stories, or even act out these imagined scenes. This activity not only nurtures their creativity, but also helps them understand character development and motivations.

STORY SETTINGS:

Dive into the settings of the books you read. If the story takes place in a unique location, research and explore real-life places that are similar. You can even plan a themed day out or a virtual tour based on the setting. For instance, if the story is set in a medieval castle, you could visit a local museum with medieval artifacts or have a castle-themed craft day at home.

BOOK-INSPIRED ARTS AND CRAFTS:

Extend the world of the story through arts and crafts. Create crafts that relate to the themes, characters, or events in the book. This hands-on approach allows your children to visualize and engage with the content in a tactile way. Whether it's making a map of the story's world, crafting masks of the characters, or building a diorama of a key scene, these activities make the story come alive.

BOOK CLUB FOR TWO:

Create a mini book club with your child. Choose a book that you both read independently, and then set aside special times to discuss what you've read. Share your thoughts, favorite parts, and even ask questions that spark meaningful conversations. This activity encourages critical thinking and analytical skills, while also strengthening your parent-child bond.

JOURNALING ADVENTURES:

Encourage your children to keep a reading journal. After each book, they can jot down their thoughts, reactions, and any new words they've learned. This practice not only helps them reflect on their reading journey, but also improves their writing skills and vocabulary.

By infusing your children's reading experiences with these engaging activities, you're opening doors to exploration, creativity, and a deeper connection with the stories they encounter. These activities not only enrich their reading journey, but also create cherished memories that will last a lifetime.

In the journey of nurturing young readers, a touch of

innovation can transform routine into adventure. By engaging the senses, exploring new reading environments, adapting to changing schedules, and fostering interactive storytelling, you're enriching your children's relationship with books. Remember, the magic of reading lies not just in the words on the page, but also in the experiences shared and memories created during these moments. So, gather your imagination, seize the opportunities, and let the "boredom bucket" be a thing of the past.

NOTES:

Key learnings from this chapter

Your Children Are Not Their Grades

My first year of college I remember observing students paying other students to write their papers. Some could barely read and others struggled with both reading and writing. Over the course of the year I watched the number of students that filled the lecture halls. Do you know what all of these students had in common? They all were accepted into the university. That means prior to the start of the year they were good students with "good grades."

I remember when my son was in 3rd grade and he came home with a failing grade on his vocabulary work. I proceeded to discuss the grade with him only to find out the work was graded incorrectly by another student. I reviewed the work with him and it was as he described. The answers he provided were correct, but the student he was asked to switch his paper with to "cross grade" marked them wrong. To make matters worse, the teacher, without checking, accepted the grades at the top of the papers. I asked my son what the teacher said when he went to dispute his grade; she said she had papers to grade and she'd talk with him "later."

I recall a doctor on my caseload while I was working as a probation/parole officer. His crime was stealing from the hospital. He stole from the hospital to support his drug habit —a drug habit he explained had started in high school. His parents, he stated, placed a great deal of pressure on him to succeed academically, which continued on into his college years. He was to follow in the footsteps of his father, who was also a doctor. He started drugs to cope and the addiction worsened in medical school.

I often hear parents mention how they do not accept anything less than an "A" or anything below an "80" on their children's reading classwork or test. The problem isn't wanting our children to perform well. The problem isn't using a letter grade or number as a measurement. The problem is lack of discernment and what we are inadvertently doing to our children, as a whole, when this is what we convey to them as "success." Here are some questions to ask yourself to avoid being the parent who only accepts "As" or tells your child with the "95" that they need to do better:

Sure your child has an "A," but do they understand what they have read and why it is important? Do they know the vocabulary and how to use it in their own sentences when spoken or written?

Will they retain what you have taught them so when it shows up again in later years or with their own children they can actually use it?

Are they able to make the lasting connection between what they learned and how to transfer that knowledge into a future job or career path?

What was the interaction with you and your child before they went to school the day of a test, or even the night before? Did you tell them to do their best, or did you threaten them that if they came home with less than a satisfactory grade they'd be on punishment for the weekend—or worse?

How do you celebrate their progress and reading successes, and how do you help them to overcome their challenges?

What are you and your child's short- and long-term reading goals?

Your children are more than their grades. Teach them that it is more productive to learn the information, make sense of it, retain it, and be able to apply it.

NOTES:

Key learnings from this chapter

Children with Disabilities Embracing Reading

Meet Emily, a loving and determined mother, as she navigates the reading journey with her son, Alex, who has autism. Their story is a testament to the power of patience, understanding, and personalized strategies that can transform challenges into moments of triumph and joy.

Emily's journey began when she noticed that Alex, age 5, had difficulty focusing on books and struggled with certain sounds and textures. Concerned, she sought advice from specialists and educators, determined to find ways to support Alex's reading experience. Armed with newfound knowledge and an unwavering commitment to her son's growth, Emily embarked on a journey that would redefine their relationship with reading.

At first, every reading session felt like a puzzle to solve. Traditional methods weren't always effective for Alex, and Emily often felt frustrated and overwhelmed. But she refused to give up. She immersed herself in research, exploring adaptive techniques and resources tailored to children with autism. She discovered that incorporating sensory elements, like soft textures or soothing scents, could engage Alex and create a more enjoyable reading environment.

Emily also realized that Alex's deep interests played a crucial role in their reading journey. She started selecting books centered around subjects Alex was passionate about—space exploration and animals. These topics sparked his curiosity and motivated him to engage with the stories. Emily saw how incorporating Alex's interests transformed reading time into an exciting adventure they could embark on together.

The breakthroughs were gradual, but they were significant. With each small triumph, Emily witnessed not only Alex's progress in reading comprehension, but also the strengthening of their bond. She celebrated when Alex read his first full sentence aloud and laughed joyfully during their imaginative discussions about aliens and jungles. Emily learned that patience and a willingness to adapt were key factors in supporting Alex's reading journey.

Through community involvement, Emily discovered local programs that provided specialized support for children with disabilities. Attending these events introduced them to other families facing similar challenges, creating a sense of belonging and shared experience. It was through these connections that Emily found solace and inspiration, realizing that she was not alone on this journey.

As the months went by, Emily's dedication and love continued to shine. She transformed reading time into an opportunity for connection, understanding, and growth. Through trial and error, she developed a repertoire of strategies that catered to Alex's needs – from incorporating visual cues to practicing patience during moments of resistance.

Emily's journey with Alex is a reminder that every child's reading journey is unique and that challenges can be transformed into moments of triumph and connection. By approaching reading with patience, understanding, and tailored strategies, parents can create an environment where their children with disabilities not only learn to read, but also discover the joy of storytelling and the wonders of imagination. Every step counts, and every effort made is a step toward fostering a love for stories that can last a lifetime.

Let's break down some of the ways you can support your child with various challenges you may be facing:

UNDERSTANDING INDIVIDUAL NEEDS:

Children with disabilities have varying strengths and challenges. Take the time to understand your child's specific needs, learning styles, and preferences. Recognize their abilities and find ways to adapt reading activities accordingly. Whether your child has a speech impairment, dyslexia, autism, or any other disability, personalized strategies can make a significant difference.

ADAPTING READING MATERIALS:

Choose books that cater to your child's interests and reading level. For children with visual impairments, opt for braille books or audio versions. E-books with adjustable font sizes and background colors can be beneficial for children with dyslexia or visual sensitivities. Some children with sensory-processing disorders may enjoy books with tactile elements or interactive features.

CREATING A COMFORTABLE ENVIRONMENT:

Reading should be a comfortable and enjoyable experience. Create a quiet, calming space where your child feels relaxed and focused. Consider sensory needs—whether it's providing fidget toys, weighted blankets, or noise-canceling headphones, tailoring the environment to your child's preferences can enhance their reading experience.

MULTI-SENSORY APPROACHES:

Many children with disabilities benefit from multi-sensory learning. Use techniques that engage multiple senses simultaneously. For example, combine reading with tactile activities, music, movement, or even aromas that align with the story. This approach can enhance comprehension and retention while making reading more engaging.

VISUAL AIDS AND SUPPORTS:

Visual aids such as visual schedules, storyboards, or picture cues can be invaluable for children with certain disabilities, helping them follow the flow of a story and anticipate transitions. Visual support can also aid in understanding and remembering new vocabulary or concepts.

REHABILITATION SPECIALIST:

Speak with your child's pediatrician, speech therapist, and other providers for suggestions on ways to best help meet your child's learning needs. In some instances they may be willing to include you in some of the sessions so that you can practice some of the strategies with support; others may come out to your home to work with you both in your own environment.

PATIENCE AND ENCOURAGEMENT:

Progress may not always follow a linear path, and that's okay. Celebrate every achievement, no matter how small. Be patient and offer plenty of encouragement. Reading might take longer or require different strategies, but your support and belief in your child's abilities are pivotal.

INCORPORATING INTERESTS:

Find ways to incorporate your child's interests into the reading experience. If your child is passionate about a specific topic, seek out books related to that interest. This not only engages them but also shows that reading can connect to their hobbies and passions.

ASSISTIVE TECHNOLOGY:

Utilize assistive technology if it's appropriate for your child. Screen readers, speech-to-text software, and specialized reading apps can be valuable tools that empower children with disabilities to access and enjoy literature.

FOSTERING A LOVE FOR STORIES:

Ultimately, the goal is to nurture a love for stories and reading. Focus on the joy of storytelling and the connection it creates between you and your child. Adapt activities, explore various formats, and embrace the ways your child engages with stories.

FIND SUPPORT:

Having a child with a learning disability can take a toll on parents. It's typically unchartered territory, and there may be times when it impacts you and your child emotionally and mentally. Take time to find a support group of other parents and children living with the same disability. Not only will it provide you with much needed support, but it also will be another way to gain insight and strategies that other parents are using to teach their kids, that in turn you can use to help yours.

Remember, you are your child's advocate and partner in this journey. Your unwavering support, adaptability, and understanding will create a foundation for a reading experience that is both meaningful and empowering. Through the pages of books, your child can embark on remarkable adventures and explore the wonders of imagination, regardless of any challenges they may face.

Notes:

Key learnings from this chapter

THE PARENT-TEACHER RELATIONSHIP

Too often when children are falling behind in reading, the parents blame the teachers and the teachers blame the parents. However, it is both parties' responsibility to see to it that children are learning to read. In the middle is the child, and they also suffer the consequences when the parent-teacher relationship is weak. Building a relationship with your child's teacher is imperative. By having open and honest conversations, you can clue them in on your child's unique learning style, what they relate well to at home, and where they might need a hand. Sharing your observations and thoughts helps teachers get what your kid needs to progress with reading. This teamwork lets teachers adjust their game plan, giving your child the extra oomph they need for their in-class reading experience. Plus, when teachers hit resource roadblocks, it can sometimes fall on parents to pick up the slack. Being ready to step up and provide a bit of extra support becomes a big deal. Parents can jazz up classroom learning with extra resources, cool reading activities at home, and a cozy reading vibe. Being ready for this helps parents add to what's happening at school, making sure their child's reading adventure keeps on the right track. By understanding that there might be some bumps along the way and working together with teachers, parents get to be the superstar backup in their child's education, ready to handle anything that pops up.

A Shared Mission with a Twist:

Parents and teachers both have one big mission: giving kids the best shot at emotional and academic success. Reading is the main event in this mission. Parents bring in the love, the cheers, and the personalized attention, while teachers show up with their expert skills, structured class setups, and smart teaching strategies.

Navigating the Classroom Dance:

Today's classrooms are like bustling marketplaces, buzzing with diverse learning styles, abilities, and cultures. These spaces embrace inclusivity, ensuring that every child's journey is valued. Amidst this mix, teachers often find themselves in a balancing act, managing a myriad of needs. But here's the kicker—sometimes, due to a lack of resources, they can't offer the individual support they want to.

In the world of education, teachers often have expectations placed on them to "do it all," crafting futures and inspiring minds. Yet, just like any champion, they, too, face their share of hurdles. Amidst the vibrant hum of today's classrooms, with their eclectic mix of student needs and aspirations, the availability of resources often runs thin. The realization that there is in fact diversity in every classroom, characterized by its diverse array of student needs and aspirations, means that the availability of resources can at times become a delicate balancing act. This scarcity may translate into a lack of sufficient time, essential supplies, or specialized support. In these instances, the noble aspiration of offering tailored, individualized attention to each child's reading journey might encounter its share of challenges.

When heroes team up, we enter the parent-teacher dynamic—a partnership that mirrors the synergy of a relay race where the baton of support is seamlessly passed between two essential figures. Parents and teachers coalesce to form a powerful duo, united by their common cause: the well-rounded growth of each child. Imagine this collaboration as a dance of shared wisdom, where parents and teachers engage in meaningful conversations, exchange insights, and collectively craft strategies. For parents, this alliance unveils the behind-the-scenes dynamics of the classroom, providing a glimpse into the learning environment. Conversely, for teachers, it offers a window into the home atmosphere, a place where a child's true essence blossoms. This dynamic duo creates an "A-team" of encouragement and support that envelops each child's learning journey with a tapestry of insights, inspiration, and the promise of an enriched reading experience.

Embracing some of your child's educational needs can definitely be a bit of a juggle, but it's all part of the adventure. Balancing the demands of daily life while sprinkling in those learning moments might seem like a puzzle at times. Yet, the cool thing is that these educational tidbits can seamlessly blend into your everyday routine. Whether it's sparking conversations during family meals, exploring nature together, or getting creative with arts and crafts, learning can be an organic part of your daily rhythm. It's like adding a dash of learning flavor to the mix, turning even the simplest activities into opportunities for growth. While it might take some tweaking and a bit of flexibility, weaving education into everyday life adds a pinch of magic to your family journey.

In the dynamic world of education, teachers encounter a

myriad of hurdles within the classroom. Navigating the diverse needs and learning styles of students, fostering a positive and inclusive environment, and delivering engaging lessons that resonate with every individual can be a complex puzzle. Moreover, managing limited resources, addressing varying levels of preparedness, and adhering to curriculum demands all add layers of complexity to their role. From addressing the emotional well-being of students to striking a balance between academic rigidity and creative expression, teachers are entrusted with the formidable task of shaping young minds amidst a sea of challenges. Despite these obstacles, teachers bring their unwavering dedication, innovative spirit, and unyielding passion to create a nurturing space where learning thrives. It's important to know your voice matters and you, too, are part of the solution. When we all work together to share strategies and support the common goal—our children —we all win.

NOTES:

Key learnings from this chapter

As a Parent Thinks,
A Child Becomes

"Sticks and stones may break my bones, but names will never hurt me." This saying is one of the worst sayings that we use to help our children cope with name-calling and the damage it can do. As a child I badly wanted to believe in this and I'm certain I may have used it on a playground as a child when bullied. When I became an adult the reality hit me: the whole saying is trash. A disservice. Parents everywhere tell this to their kids as a quick fix. It takes the responsibility off of the parent from actually addressing the situation, and the innocent kid believes it and all is supposed to be right with the world. The reality is words do hurt and depending on who the words are coming from, it stings and can have lasting effects. Don't believe me, take some time and look up "verbal abuse and childhood trauma." You know what else is overlooked? The fact that every joke contains some form of truth. That's right, so saying this in a "joking" way to kids is equally damaging, not humorous, and kids deep down know when a joke is backhanded. Being a parent places us in a unique position to either be the one dishing out the name-calling, put downs and ill-intentioned jokes or being our child's biggest support, personal cheerleader, encourager, and protector.

When being taught to read, our kids at any given time can be filled with various emotions concerning the subject. They also, on any given day, show up as human beings, meaning that they, too, can be coming to the learning table unhappy, discouraged, resistant, and feeling bad about themselves and their abilities. As parents, even on our worst days, we have a responsibility to show up as their unwavering anchor.

We may be stressed about the events of our day prior to working with our kids, we still may be upset about how dreadfully the last reading session went, we may be frustrated with our kids or with ourselves, and the list goes on. However, we have to check our baggage at the learning door. More importantly, we have to show our kids how to do the same.

Whether we like it or not, when we are teaching our kids to read, there is an exchange of information and an exchange of energy. We can show up to exchange reading knowledge, but if the energy is strained, low or negative, nothing productive is going to be accomplished. No matter what you think, what your children say, or what other adults have shared with you, know this: what you think of your child and what you say to your child matter!

Most importantly, it matters to your kids. You then have two choices: you can speak to them and of them in ways that build them up or beat them down. Sometimes the reading journey comes to a dead end not because of the reading or the books but because of the parent-child relationship.

Some of you have children who have already decided that they don't want anything to do with reading because they equate it with the negative interaction they have with their parents surrounding the reading lessons. Before they've sat down with you to read or study, they already tapped out mentally. They showed up because they have to and they just want to get it over with. No joy, no effort, no learning taking place—just dread, anxiousness and/or hurt. Below are tips to avoid and get yourself out of this kind of parent-child dynamic.

AFFIRM YOURSELF FIRST

If you've ever taken a flight, you know that when they review how to utilize your face mask for emergencies, they tell parents to put their mask on first then their child's. The reason being, if you don't have oxygen for yourself while attempting to save your child, then you're not going to be of any use to yourself or your child. The same applies to teaching your kid to read. Make sure you're well rested, calm, and in a good mood. Speak positively to yourself, say things like "I got this," "I'm capable, loving, and strong," "This is about quality, not quantity," "Some reading is better than no reading," "My child and I are perfectly unique. We are not our mistakes. We are not other people," "Today is a new day," "I am exactly who my child needs," and "I am phenomenal." You can feel free to add to this list.

Affirm Your Child

Children need affirming often, no matter how young they are. From babies to young adults, they are looking for cues from their environments and the people within them to learn about themselves. Sometimes the feedback is confusing and sometimes it isn't kind. As their parents, be consistent and positive. Compliment them, tell them you're proud of them and that you love them. Congratulate them for their wins and for the times they are brave and do their best. Acknowledge their weird but individual style, their good decision making and, most importantly, the effort they put into their learning and reading. Say things like, "I know you'd rather do anything else but reading right now. I admire that you're here, sticking with it and knowing that we're in this together," "Look at the progress you made," and "Let's talk about what you're doing well and what you learned from errors this week."

Showcase Their Work

Remember those art projects or medals you won as a kid for some achievement you attained? Now remember how proud you were and excited you felt to present them to someone in your family? Looking back as adults we may laugh at how hideous those art projects were or how silly the medal was for best student chalkboard eraser, but at that moment when we were kids, they were a huge deal. The icing on the cake was the smile on our parents' faces and them telling us how happy they were to receive such things from us. As kids it was the ultimate. It felt good to know our family loved us, thought we did good work, and were good people. Your kids need those moments, too. When they bring you artwork they're proud of, even if you can't really identify it, hang it up where everyone can see. Hang the test and written papers with C grades if they are improvements from the last one. Let them hear you talking positively to other friends and family about them—not just how well they did something, but also their efforts and how they improved on their mistakes. Applaud their courage when they dare to try something new or attempt to figure something out for themselves. It will encourage more positive behavior.

AFFECTION

When your kid is struggling or you both had a tough reading moment, tell them you love them, give them a hug or say something funny to lighten the mood. Reading and learning should not be a duel between you and your child; you're on the same team. Showing you love them no matter how hard it gets or how angry they become goes a long way. It says "No matter what, WE are going to get through this," and "I got you."

BREAK THE ICE

I encourage snacks when studying. First of all, a good snack or a kid's favorite snack lightens the mood. Second, it's a good distraction and anxiety reducer. When kids are eating snacks when reading or studying it gives their hands something to do and heightens the senses. Last, if your kid is hungry, there is something at their fingertips. A kid who is hungry cannot concentrate.

END WITH KINDNESS

If things went well, tell them so, and if things didn't go well, discuss together what you both want to do to improve the next time.

NOTES:

Key learnings from this chapter

If Not You,
Then Who?

Years ago during a parent-teacher conference, I inquired about the selection of books the teacher was using. She walked with me to the back of her classroom and pointed to an old, worn-out collection of books. With a look of disappointment on her face she turned to me and said "These are the books we are required to use in the classroom. I personally wouldn't use them to teach our students, but I have no choice. I suggest you continue to use other books on your son's reading level to help improve his reading skills."

At a high-school open house I visited a classroom where the textbooks were kept in the closet. When I asked the teacher if they were the textbooks the students would be using that year he replied, "Oh no, those are old and not of much use so they stay in the closet. I make copies from other texts to teach the students." In my mind all I envisioned was teachers who had their hands tied by dated school-system policies and curricula, with students at an extreme disadvantage.

If we as parents believe that our kids "will learn it at school," we are sadly mistaken. When the books are outdated and teachers have to adhere to strict curricula and rules surrounding the books that they can use, how can they be relied on to be the persons solely responsible to adequately teach your child? In the event that they do, there is the risk that it's "watered down" and surface-level.

As a parent, you are your child's first and most influential teacher. Your involvement in their learning journey can make a profound difference in their ability to read and, ultimately, succeed in life. However, it's not uncommon for parents to grapple with doubts and imposter syndrome when it comes to teaching their children how to read. You might find yourself wondering, "Am I qualified? Can I really do this?" The truth is, you absolutely can, and this chapter is here to help you overcome those feelings of self-doubt and equip you with the confidence and strategies needed to be an effective reading mentor for your child.

EMBRACING YOUR ROLE

Teaching your child to read is a profoundly personal journey, and it's crucial to recognize that you bring something truly unique to the table as a parent. You don't need a formal teaching degree to make a significant impact on your child's literacy development.

Your deep, emotional connection with your child is an invaluable asset. You know them better than anyone else. You've witnessed their growth, celebrated their achievements, and comforted them during moments of frustration. This bond, built on love and trust, is the foundation upon which effective teaching is built.

Imagine this: you're aware of their favorite stories, the characters they adore, and the topics that ignite their curiosity. You can see the sparkle in their eyes when they're engaged in something they love, and you're attuned to the signs of when they need a little encouragement. This intimate knowledge allows you to craft a learning experience tailored specifically to them.

Every child is unique, and there is no universal formula for teaching reading that fits every child's needs. Your approach can be fluid and adaptable, responding to your child's individual requirements. Whether your child is a visual learner, a hands-on explorer, or a curious questioner, you have the capacity to tailor your methods to their learning style.

Perhaps your child is eager to devour books, or maybe they're taking a more cautious approach to reading. Regardless of the pace at which they progress, your role as a guide is to provide unwavering support. Your love and encouragement will serve as a constant source of motivation, reassuring your child that they have a dedicated champion by their side.

In essence, teaching your child to read is not about following a strict curriculum or adhering to someone else's checklist. It's about recognizing the special connection you share, understanding your child's uniqueness, and allowing that knowledge to inform your teaching approach. You are their guiding light on this exciting journey into the world of literacy, and your love and support are the most powerful tools you possess.

Conquering Imposter Syndrome

Imposter syndrome, that nagging feeling that you're not qualified or capable enough to teach your child to read, can be a formidable obstacle. It's common to doubt your abilities, especially when you lack formal training in education. But here's the reassuring truth: you don't need a teaching degree to foster a deep love of reading in your child. What truly matters are qualities like dedication, patience, and a willingness to learn together.

In this journey, it's important to embrace the fact that you won't have all the answers. None of us do, and that's perfectly okay. In fact, it's this shared learning experience that can be incredibly beautiful and strengthen the bond you share with your child.

Picture this: as you embark on the adventure of reading together, you both encounter new words, stories, and ideas. You stumble upon words neither of you has heard before, and together, you explore their meanings. You might come across a story that challenges both of you, sparking thoughtful discussions and encouraging critical thinking. In these moments of discovery, your role shifts from being the all-knowing teacher to being a curious learner alongside your child.

Don't hesitate to seek out resources that can provide guidance and support in this journey. There's a wealth of books, websites, and educational apps available to help both you and your child. These tools can serve as valuable companions on your reading adventure, offering fresh ideas, interactive activities, and a myriad of stories to explore together.

Consider attending workshops or parent-teacher meetings at your child's school. These gatherings can be valuable opportunities to gain insights from experienced educators who are well-versed in teaching reading. They can offer tips, strategies, and a deeper understanding of how children learn to read, enriching your own teaching approach.

In essence, don't let imposter syndrome hold you back. You may not have a formal teaching degree, but you possess the essential qualities required to nurture a love of reading in your child. By acknowledging that learning together is a beautiful and rewarding journey, seeking out resources, and connecting with educators, you're equipping yourself with the tools you need to guide your child toward a lifelong love of reading.

Navigating Your Own Challenges

It's entirely possible that you might not consider yourself a confident reader. Perhaps you faced challenges with reading during your own childhood, or life circumstances didn't afford you the opportunity to develop strong reading skills. But remember, your own reading journey should never deter you from guiding your child towards success in reading.

Instead, view this situation as a unique opportunity for both you and your child to learn and grow together. Embrace the idea that reading is not just a destination, but rather a continuous journey. As you venture into the world of books with your child, do so at your own pace. Reading is not a race; it's a lifelong pursuit of knowledge, imagination, and personal growth.

Consider reaching out for support when needed. Teachers, librarians, and local literacy programs are valuable resources that can offer guidance and assistance. They can help you navigate any challenges you encounter and provide suggestions for age-appropriate books that cater to your child's interests and reading level.

Your willingness to confront your own reading challenges head-on is a powerful example for your child. It demonstrates that learning is a journey filled with ups and downs, setbacks and successes. By showing your child that it's okay to seek help, to persevere through difficulties, and to continually strive for improvement, you impart essential life lessons beyond the realm of reading. You teach them resilience, determination, and the value of seeking knowledge throughout their lives.

In essence, your personal experiences with reading should not be a barrier to guiding your child on their own reading journey. Embrace the opportunity to learn and grow together, and let your commitment to lifelong learning be a shining example for your child, showing them that with perseverance and support, they can overcome any challenges they may face on their path to becoming confident readers.

If not you, then who? Your involvement in your child's reading development is irreplaceable. Embrace your role as a parent-teacher, conquer imposter syndrome, and don't let your own reading struggles hold you back. Your child's literacy journey is a shared adventure, and together, you can unlock a world of knowledge, imagination, and endless possibilities through the magic of reading.

NOTES:

Key learnings from this chapter

A WORLD WITHOUT READING

One of the aims of juvenile correctional facilities is to educate children whether they are awaiting the outcome of their charges or already sentenced. Many of the youth range in age from 12-19. They receive testing and evaluations, and they are then placed into the appropriate classes. Some receive their GED and take first-year college classes. The goal is to help them continue their education while incarcerated and, in some instances, improve their learning abilities and grades so they can graduate to the next grade level. The school setting in corrections can come with some of the same challenges that the kids face on the outside. Fights, refusal to complete work, arguments with teachers, and simply having to get in the habit of attending daily can take place on any given day.

I remember one student who was put out of class at least once a day for conflicts with teachers and his peers. After many days of observing the situation, I asked him what was causing him to act out and be sent to detention. He said "I don't read well and the other kids make jokes about it. When it's time for me to read I start a fight so I can be sent out of class and not have to read."

Stories like the student's above are common at all grade levels. My son once told me about an English class in which the teacher spent the entire class sending a kid back and forth to the principal's office. No sooner than he was disruptive and sent out, the principal would send him back to class and the disruptive cycle would start all over again. By the time class was over the rest of the students left the class without having reviewed the reading for that day.

My aunt, who taught high-school students for years, informed me that the majority of students in her special-education class were not in special education. They were the students whom the teachers had difficulty keeping engaged, so behaviors ensued that they did not want to deal with, thus the students were labeled "special education," and special education was where they stayed.

According to BeginToRead.com, "Some 85% of youth who are involved in the juvenile court system are classified as functionally illiterate. About 70% of inmates in the U.S. prisons can't read above a fourth-grade level." The school-to-prison pipeline consists of school practices and policies that serve to push students out of school into the prison system. "Zero tolerance" policies; schools that are disproportionately suspending African-Americans, Latinos, and children from low-socioeconomic backgrounds; and increased police presence in schools all contribute to the school-to-prison pipeline. Investing in the criminalization of students rather than in the resources and support these children need to succeed in school places them at an increased risk for prison.

How does reading tie in? A child who cannot read or reads poorly becomes an adult who cannot read. Without reading, adults cannot obtain employment, leading to a life of poverty and crime. Children who are criminalized tend to be labeled and bullied in school by teachers and peers, and thus do not feel welcomed, which leads them to spend more time skipping school and being in the streets where their chances of getting involved in criminal activity increase.

There is a direct connection between children who cannot read and prison. This does not mean your struggling reader is doomed for a life of crime and prison; it means that without reading, the chances of prison increase. This is also to point out that if you were depending on the teachers and the school system as the sole providers of your child's reading education, this is your reason to step up and change your mentality.

NOTES:

Key learnings from this chapter

THANK YOU

If you have enjoyed or found value in this book, please take a moment to leave an honest/brief review on <u>Amazon</u> **amzn. to/3QXNp14** or <u>Goodreads</u> . Your reviews help prospective readers decide if this is right for them & it is the greatest kindness you can offer the author.

Thank you in advance.

About the Author

HEADSHOT

Michelle Gomes is a loving mother, registered nurse, children's book author, and an advocate for closing the reading gap among children. She is the author of *Orsa and the Three Brothers* book and workbook, as well as her upcoming book, *Space Adventure*.

Reading and writing were two of her favorite pastimes as a child, and she dreamed that one day she would create her own magazine for which she would be a contributing writer. In 2019 she was inspired to start writing again because she recognized a need for educational children's books that her children, and other African American children, could see themselves in. She hopes that her books help children develop a love of reading and learning.

Michelle has a B.A in Criminal Justice from Temple

University and a B.S. in Nursing from Salve Regina University. She currently lives in Rhode Island, where she enjoys the beaches, fresh seafood, and spending time with her three children, family, and friends.

Want some free resources for you and your child(ren)? Check out Michelle's site for free resources.

levels2learning.com/free-resources

instagram.com/levels_2_learn

Space Venture

Beginner readers will enjoy this informational text about the planets. Colorfully illustrated, written in rhyme, filled with facts and basic vocabulary this book follows two young characters on their journey to the eight planets. Readers will have fun finding out who and what the characters run into along the way.

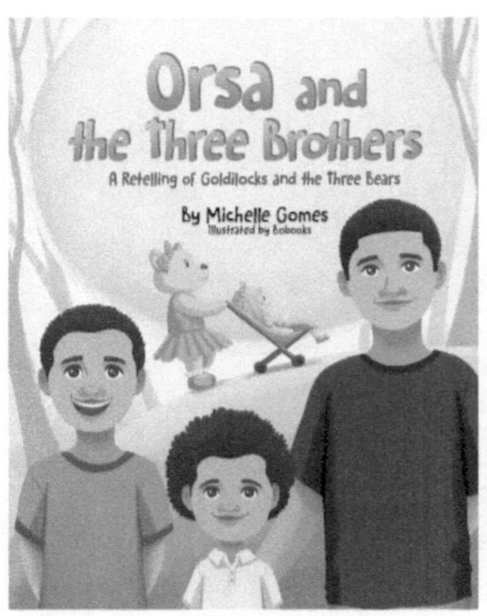

Orsa And The Three Brothers!

Find out what happens when three brothers get an unexpected visit from Orsa, a young bear, who enters their home without permission. This is a new twist on the old tale Goldilocks and the Three Bears.

Orsa And The Three Brothers! Workbook

Companion workbook for "The Three Brothers: A Retelling of Goldilocks and the Three Bears" Students grades K-3 will complete reading curriculum activities related to the story and aligned with the state common core standards for reading literature.

levels2learning.com/our-shop

The Story of
Levels2Learning

Levels2Learning was established in 2019 by owner Michelle Gomes to meet the need for relatable, relevant and fun educational books and products that are inclusive of African Americans. There are plenty of programs, institutions and organizations working tirelessly to raise the educational standards for African American children, however, the lack of relatable, relevant, and fun educational content for these children continues to be a barrier to meeting the expectations of such efforts.

OUR VISION

We deal in numerous products such as children's books, workbooks, flashcards, digital downloads, school supplies, toys, clothing and other educational resources focusing on representing African Americans, their lived experiences, stories, and contributions to the world. Doing so enables us to reach our vision of raising the educational standards of African American children and other children as well. Our highly curated educational resources strive to overcome the learning and reading gap prevalent in the US. Our vision is to create a highly inclusive society of diverse and capable individuals that all come together to benefit humankind.

OUR VISION

In simple words, Levels2Learning is a one-stop education solution for homeschooling families, teachers, parents, and students seeking educational books and products inclusive of African Americans.

How does it Work?

At Levels2Learning, we have come up with a two-pronged solution to achieve our vision and mission. It is also the reason why we chose the name we chose. At the very core, it starts with a simple formula. A formula that has proven to be useful and effective time and again. It is natural for children to understand better what they can relate to. Their minds are more stimulated when they are taught in a fun, relevant, and relatable manner.

All our educational resources, teaching methods, and learning materials are created on this premise.

We create lessons, stories, and content for African American children that are fascinating and inspiring to them. All these resources relate to children's experiences and the aspirations they hold close to their hearts. Moreover, such content represents the true themes of African American life and highlights the issues, challenges, and solutions in an easy-to-understand manner.

Doing so lets us impact children's psychology in such a manner that they grow up with ...

- a strong sense of their African American identity .
- a deeper understanding of themselves .
- a desire to create solutions for themselves, others, their communities and the world.

When children learn who their heroes are, what their struggles are, and what's important to their community in a fun and engaging manner, they grow up with a conviction of doing something about it.It might seem far-fetched, but this will create a generation of intelligent and confident individuals who will strive to change the world for the better.

But that's just one prong of Levels2Learning. What's the second one?

Education is not limited to institutions, buildings, or premises such as schools, colleges, or universities. In its truest sense, education is a constant and consistent process that happens to children wherever they happen to be. They observe and learn from everything around them.

At Levels2Learning, our products are as effective and useful for children learning at schools as they are for children learning at home. To ensure total inclusivity, we create our products with all kinds of children in mind, whether they are homeschooled or otherwise.

By doing so, we ensure that no child is deprived of what we aim to impart and what we stand for at Levels2Learning.

Diverse & Inclusive Flashcards: Verbs

Each flashcard set includes:

- 50 Flashcards
- Each flashcard has a picture on the front and a sentence on the back
- Verbs are in bold
- Sentences feature words from Dolch and Fry vocabulary list
- Pictures are of persons from different races, cultures, ages and varying abilities
- Use pictures with or without the sentences as a teaching tool
- For, but not limited to, grades
- K-3, beginner readers, and ESL students

Red Thread Publishing

Red Thread Publishing is an all-female publishing company on a mission to support 10,000 women to become successful published authorpreneurs & thought leaders.

To work with us or connect regarding any of our growing library of books email us at **info@redthreadbooks.com.**

To learn more bout us visit our website **www.redthreadbooks.com.**

Follow us & join the community.

facebook.com/redthreadpublishing

instagram.com/redthreadbooks

www.ingramcontent.com/pod-product-compliance
Lightning Source LLC
Chambersburg PA
CBHW021329060726
47591CB00006B/1935